Not Another Money Statistic:

Lessons We Wish We Learned in High School

Alli Rosenblum & Shelly Hawkins

www.financiallifocused.com/nams

Cover Design: Armend Meha

ISBN-13: 978-0-692-13204-3

First Edition
Printed in the United States

DISCLAIMER

Everything shared in this book is intended for informational purposes only based on what has worked for us. This book contains personal opinions, experiences, conversations with friends, and personal research. While all attempts are made to present accurate information, information may become outdated over time. We hope this book helps you become more financially savvy.

Although we try to bring accurate information, under no circumstances can or do we warrant the completeness or accuracy of the content found in this book, or its usefulness for any particular purpose. Therefore, we make absolutely no promises or warranties, nor accept responsibility for any liability, injury or damage that you may cause or incur when using the information provided in this book. You are responsible for your own decisions. We hope we can help avoid becoming another money statistic.

TABLE OF CONTENTS

Part Three: Life After High School

Appendix

ACKNOWLEDGMENTS

Thanks to our wonderful families for always supporting us. We know we've caused you a lot of anxiety over the years, but we wouldn't be where we are today without your support. From hitchhiking in Costa Rica to surviving spontaneous adventures in Nicaragua, we promise this next endeavor will be our best yet (and a lot safer).

To our moms, you can now post on Facebook how your daughters are authors.

To the University of South Carolina, thanks for bringing us together.

INTRODUCTION

Did you know most high schools do not teach personal finance? We learn calculus and the periodic table but do not learn how to stay out of debt and how to create a budget.

You might be sitting here thinking, oh this won't be me but without the tools and knowledge it might be you. We have compiled what we have learned to help you avoid mistakes we made and prosper financially. You also might be thinking, I am not even 20 I don't need to worry about my finances. That couldn't be further from the truth. The earlier you start thinking about your finances and preparing for the future, the better off you will be. It doesn't matter if you were prom king/queen or if you were the most popular guy/girl in school, that won't help you stay out of debt.

We promise to keep each chapter short, sweet, and

to the point. We aren't trying to bore you. We want to help set you up for success. Sounds cheesy but it's true. There are a million money books out there so why did we write one? Well many of them are geared toward fixing your money mistakes. We don't want to help fix money mistakes, we want to prevent them.

If you enjoyed this book, share it with your friends. Spread our message. Leave us a review on Amazon. We want to hear about your journey and how we can help you.

Make sure to sign up for updates on our website (www.financiallifocused.com/nams) so you will be notified when we launch future products, courses, and workshops. This book isn't the end for financial knowledge. It is just the beginning. Not Another Money Statistic is developing online courses with worksheets, videos, and tips that you can complete at your own pace so you can practice what we preach.

This is a long enough intro so let's get started. Put away your cell phone (I know you are currently scrolling on social media) or turn off Netflix/Hulu and jump right in.

WHY YOU SHOULD CARE ABOUT PERSONAL FINANCE

I bet if you made a list of things that are important to you, personal finance might be pretty low on the list (if it is on the list at all). I get it; you are young and you have more important things to worry about like hanging with your friends or who you are going to take to prom. I've been there too. When I was in high school, I definitely was not thinking about high-yield savings accounts or creating a budget.

High school is a time to grow, learn, and start becoming an adult. High school will end and everyone will move on to bigger and better things. Learning how to manage your money now will allow you to lead the lifestyle you want instead of the one you can afford. Effectively managing your money is one of the things that will set you apart at your 10, 20 or even 30-year high school reunion.

Maybe you don't care about your high school reunion, but here are some reasons why you should care about personal finance:

1. Your parents (most likely) won't pay for your bills after high school or college so you are going to have to learn how to budget.

2. Living within your means allows you to splurge on the things that matter to you.

3. You'll be able to save for that spring break or summer trip with your friends.

4. So you can pick a job you love instead of a job you need because you need the money.

5. Living paycheck to paycheck can be stressful.

6. You'll have more options for your future like retiring early, buying a house or traveling the world.

7. Being financially responsible now will help you pay for emergencies later without going into debt.

PART ONE: THE BASICS

1. CHECKING ACCOUNT

In 2015, there were approximately 15.6 million Americans living without a checking or savings account.

Do you have a place to hold your money so that you are not sleeping with a stack of cash under your pillow? If not, you need to open a checking account. It might look cool in music videos or on Instagram to have $1,000 in cash to wave around, but in reality all of those rappers, YouTuber stars and influencers keep the majority of their money in checking or savings accounts. Not to mention, keeping cash in a non-secure location is just asking for trouble. Banks can protect your money and even have insurance to cover you if anything were to happen.

Why Do I Need a Checking Account?

I can just use cash for everything, right? Wrong. If

you want to have a debit card, you need a checking account. If you want to be able to write checks, you need a checking account. If you want to get paid by direct deposit, you need a checking account. Are you sensing a trend here? Checking accounts make everything easier. It is easier to get paid, pay bills, buy things online and manage your money when you have a checking account.

Pretty much all banks and financial institutions have an online portal. Without a checking account, it is pretty difficult to exist in modern America. Companies like Venmo, Uber, Amazon and Grubhub are not going to provide products or services to you under the assumption that you will hand them an envelope of cash when they arrive. You have to link a checking account or a debit/credit card to those accounts. They don't have time for that. They are a business and they care most about being paid.

So What Is a Debit Card?

A debit card is literally a smart piece of plastic. Your debit card is connected directly to your checking account. It is NOT a credit card. You can only spend up to the amount you have available in your checking account or there will be consequences. You must keep track of your account balance. No excuses. You can sign up for online banking and keep track of all of your spending.

Most major banks have phone apps these days, so you can look at your balance right on your phone.

Overdraft Will Make You Pay

I mentioned earlier that there will be consequences if you spend more than your available balance on your debit card. That is not just a scare tactic that your parents use. Many banks will charge you an extra $35 dollars when you buy something with your debit card and you don't have the funds in your account to cover it. This is called an overdraft fee. Basically, the bank is charging you for covering you on your purchase. So let me break it down for you:

If you go to Starbucks to buy a $5 latte, but you only have $3 in your account, the bank will cover your purchase. You can have your latte! Yay! You have now bought a $40 latte because the bank will charge you a $35 overdraft fee. Plus you still have to pay the $2 you didn't have in the first place.

Which Bank Should I Use?

There are so many banks out there that it can be overwhelming to decide which one to use. I recommend looking for banks that offer free student checking accounts. Some banks will charge you for using their services, but you should not have to pay a fee. Some banks that offer free student checking as of 2018 are:

TD Bank:
- Student Checking Account for students under the age of 24
- No minimum daily balance or minimum initial deposit is required

Bank of America Core Checking:
- No monthly fee for students under 24 who are enrolled in high school, college or vocational school
- A $25 opening deposit is required

Navy Federal Credit Union:
- The Campus Checking Account is free for full-time students from 14 to 24 years of age
- There is no minimum balance or minimum deposit required
- Up to $10 in ATM fees are reimbursed

Virtual Student Wallet by PNC Bank:
- No monthly service fee or minimum balance requirement for active students
- There's a $25 initial deposit if opened in person, $0 if opened online

US Bank Student Checking:
- No monthly maintenance fee if you switch to online statements upon signing up
- $25 minimum opening deposit

Wells Fargo Teen Checking:
- For teens 13–17 who have an adult co-owner
- $25 minimum opening deposit
- The $3 monthly fee will be waived when you change to online statements

Some basic terms you need to know when opening an account are:

Minimum Initial/Opening Deposit: How much money you need to put into your account when you open it.

Minimum Balance: The amount of money you need in your account daily to avoid fees.

Monthly Maintenance/Service Fee: The fee the bank charges you for using their services.

If you are under 18, you will need your parents' help to open a bank account. Most likely, your parents will be co-owners of your account, which means they can log into your account and monitor your spending. Spend wisely.

If you are planning to move to another city or state for college, then you should make sure the bank you choose has branches in both your hometown and college town. After college, I moved to another state that did not have my bank. I started babysitting and made a bunch of cash but could never deposit it into my account. I had cash hidden all over my tiny apartment. I ended up having to open a second account, which made things very confusing. If I had known, I would have planned ahead and found a different bank.

Take Action

If you don't already have a checking account, meet with your parents to decide which bank will be the best option for you.

Checks Are for Old People

Most people don't use checks daily. There are still some people who use checks to pay at the grocery store, but that number is preetttyyy small. We have become a very automated and fast-paced society. There are some old-school businesses and organizations out there that will only accept checks. I could literally go for months without using a check, but I still need them every once in a while. Learning how to write a check is a part of becoming an adult. It is a rite of passage.

Checks work like debit cards in the fact that the funds will be taken directly out of your checking account. However, they may not be taken out immediately. It depends on when the person or business cashes/deposits the check. It is important to take this into account when looking at your checking account balance. You always need to make sure that you have enough money available in your account to cover the check so that your check doesn't "bounce". If your check "bounces" meaning you did not have enough money available in your checking account, you will have to pay an extra fee.

For example, you write a check of $100 to your school for your graduation kit on January 1st. However, the school gives everyone two months to turn in their money and so they don't deposit the checks until they have all been turned in. Your check does not get deposited into the school's account until March 1st. This means that you will have to maintain that $100 in your checking account for two months. Do you see how easy it would be to forget that you owe that money to the school? Just because you have written a check does not mean that the money has been taken from your account.

Writing a check is pretty simple. The first thing that you should always do is fill in the date that you are writing the check (A). This does matter so don't leave it blank. It will help you in the future if you ever need to figure out why or when you wrote the check. Next you need to fill "Pay to the order of" (B). This is just a fancy way of saying who this money is for. If you are paying a person, write their name. If you are paying a business, write the business name. In the box (C) fill in the dollar amount in numbers. Then, on the long line underneath (D), write out the amount in words. For example, $135 would be written as one hundred thirty-five. If there is change then you would need to write the change as a fraction over 100. For example, $135.63 would be written as one hundred thirty-five and 63/100. Lastly, you will need to sign the check (E). Yes, sign. So please learn how to at least write your full name in cursive. I know they don't teach this in many schools anymore so if you never learned ask your parents for help or watch YouTube videos.

You may be asked for your bank's routing number (F) and your account number (G) when setting up direct deposits for work, paying bills, or connecting your checking account to apps. The easiest place to find this is on your personal checks.

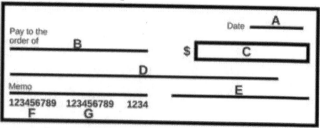

You have probably heard your parents or grandparents talking about balancing their checkbook—that is totally cool! It means that they are being responsible with their finances. However, nowadays there is a much easier way to keep up with the amount in your checking account. It's called banking or budgeting apps. Please download the app to your bank so that you can keep up with your checks and debit card purchases. If you can't download phone apps, make sure to log on your bank website at least once a week to make sure you have enough money in your checking account.

Opening a checking account is the starting point for being responsible with your finances. You will need a checking account after high school so it is important to get comfortable with it now.

2. SAVINGS

44% of adults stated that they would either have to sell something, borrow money or could not cover the expense at all if they needed $400 for an emergency.

Do you want to buy a car in the future? Maybe a house? Or maybe you want to go on a trip to Asia? Unless you win the lottery or inherit a ton of money, you will need to save for these purchases. A savings account is a place to hold your money to save for future events (car, pets, doctor, emergency, etc.). You should think of your savings account as your "hands off" account, meaning that the money there is not meant to be spent on a daily basis. Your savings account is separate from your checking account so you should not include your savings in your spending budget.

Why Should I Open a Savings Account?

There are two main reasons why you should be putting money into a savings account. The first is to save up for something that you plan to do or purchase in the future. This could be something as simple as your significant other's birthday gift or as massive as your college tuition. The money you put in your savings account should not be spent unless you have thought long and hard about spending it. You should never take money from your savings account for a spur of the moment purchase because you might regret it later. Let's be serious, you really don't need those $120 Nike shoes or the latest $200 gaming system. Remember to ask yourself when taking money from your savings account, *Is this purchase necessary? Is it going to improve my life?*

Take Action
List the things you want to buy; check back in a few months to decide if you still want them. Ask yourself, Is it necessary? Will it improve my life? Can it wait?

The second reason why you should be putting money in your savings account is for emergencies. Everyone should have an emergency fund that they can use in case of a REAL emergency. You might be thinking, *I'm in high school, why would I need an emergency fund?* Don't expect your parents to always be there to bail you out when you mess up. At some point they are going to hold you responsible.

Picture this: you are out with friends, driving your parents' car. You are jamming out and hit a light pole when leaving the parking lot. You now owe $300 to your parents for repairs. Or you are at school texting in the bathroom. The bell rings and you drop your $700 iPhone in the toilet. Your parents say that if you want a new phone, you have to pay for it yourself.

Setting up an emergency fund might not sound cool, but it is the responsible thing to do (and will impress the girls/guys in the future I promise). Believe me, at some point you are going to need it.

At this point in your life could you afford to pay a $400 emergency expense? 44% of adults stated that they would either have to sell something, borrow money or could not cover the expense at all if they needed $400 for an emergency. Don't be this statistic. Start saving early.

What Is Good Interest?

One of the main reasons why you should keep the money that you are saving in a savings account instead of a checking account is for the (good) interest. Interest is money that the bank pays you for allowing them to loan your money out to other people. Don't freak out. Your money will still be available whenever you need it. Banks work with millions and millions of dollars and clients so they know how to work the system.

So how does interest work? Each bank sets their own interest rate. Interest rates are always listed as percentages. This means that they will pay you X% of your total savings (split into monthly payments). The bank will deposit the interest directly into your savings account as payment for loaning them your money. You, personally, don't have to do anything to earn interest on your savings account. Some banks compound daily and others compound monthly. Some bigger banks have really low interest rates (.01%) and others have really high interest rates (1.5%).

For example, if you had $1000 in your savings account and your interest rate was 10% (this is REALLY high for a normal savings account but it is just an example to prove a point) then you would earn $100 per year. This means that you would earn $8.33 per month in interest. After the first month of earning interest, you would have $1008.33 in your account so your interest would be calculated based on that amount for the next month.

Month	Interest	Total Amount
0	-	$1,000
1	$8.33	$1,008.33
2	$8.40	$1,016.73
3	$8.47	$1,025.20

Take Action

This is a basic interest calculation. Calculate how much interest you would earn per month if you had an interest rate of 5% and $100 in savings. Now calculate how much interest you would earn per month if the interest rate was 10%. Which interest rate would you prefer?

Savings	Interest	Annual Interest	Monthly Interest
$100	5%	$	$
$100	10%	$	$

In this instance a higher interest rate is good because you will earn more money. However, you will learn in later chapters that high interest rates are not always good. It is important to always pay attention to interest rates and to know the difference between earning interest and paying interest. Savings accounts allow you to earn interest so you can consider it "good interest".

Calculating interest rates can be really confusing and to be honest it is not always necessary. The two most important things for you to remember in regards to interest in a savings account are:

- The more money you have in your account the more interest you will earn.
- The higher the interest rate the more money you will earn.

How Much Money Should I Deposit in My Savings Account?

This will be different for everyone, but one thing will remain the same: Every time you earn money you should put a portion of that money into your savings account. This includes birthday, Christmas and graduation money. It also includes babysitting money and money that you earn from a part-time job. Just because you have it doesn't mean you should spend it. Do I need to repeat myself?

You need to decide what your savings goals are. If you are saving for a prom dress/tux, how much does it cost and how many months do you have to save up for it? If you are creating an emergency fund for when you go off to college, how much do you need and how many months are there until you go to college? Once you set your savings goal, you will be able to decide how much to keep and how much you can spend.

Take Action

Brainstorm possible savings goals. Talk it over with your parents and pick one goal that you would like to focus on. Calculate how much money you will need to put into your savings account each month or after Christmas, birthdays and graduation.

Which Bank Should I Use?

The bank that you chose for your checking account will most likely also have a free option for a savings account. If you decide to use the same bank, then you will be able to link your accounts to easily transfer money from your checking account to your savings account. All of your accounts will also use the same online banking site or app, which makes it very simple to keep track of your finances.

If you are interested in finding a different bank for your savings account, then you should look for the following:

- No monthly fees (Free!)
- A high interest rate (1% or more)
- No minimum balance required

How Do I Open a Savings Account?

If you are under the age of 18, you will need your parent to help you open a savings account. If you already have a bank for your checking account, then you can contact them to find out if they offer a free savings account for students. If you don't already have a checking account, you can still open a savings account. You and your parent can go speak with a banker at a local bank to set up your account.

Saving money is not fun or glamorous. It might not make you look cool or impress your friends. But it does protect you. It protects you from getting into credit card debt because you had an emergency to pay for. It protects your future and your dreams because you were smart enough to plan ahead. It protects you from getting into a lot of debt that most people struggle to recover from. Start getting in the habit of saving early so that you are prepared for the ups and downs of the life ahead of you.

3. DEBT

In November 2017, the US consumer debt total rose to $3.927 trillion.

What Is Debt?

The formal definition of debt is the amount of money borrowed by one party from another. It is just money you owe someone else. This could be a bank, family member, hospital or friend.

There are many types of debt but the most common types are:
- Mortgage
- Car loan
- Credit card debt
- Student loan debt
- Medical debt
- Personal loans
- Payday loans

Obviously, in high school you don't need to worry about a mortgage, but it is important to understand the different types of debt. You most likely will experience at least a few of these. I won't go into detail about all of them, but there are some you 100% should try to avoid at all costs.

The main one you should ALWAYS try to avoid is payday loans. You probably see these companies when you're driving around your town. They are everywhere, especially since the debt crisis in the United States is insane. The main problem with payday loans is they carry extremely high interest rates. They seem appealing because they have great marketing tactics and offer fast cash, but please avoid them at all costs.

We will talk about credit cards in the next chapter and student loans in another section, so I won't go into detail here. The most important takeaway is there are many types of debt and it is important to understand what you are getting yourself into before you take on any debt. Don't take the decision lightly.

Why Should I Care?

Although you might not have debt now, you might not even have a job, you will be faced with important money decisions in the future. You might decide to take out student loans to pay for college, open a credit card or even buy a house. You need to weigh the pros and cons of taking on the debt and completely understand the terms. I want to make sure you are prepared to take on the debt and understand what you are signing up for.

Debt affects everyone. If you are one of the super lucky ones who stays debt free it will affect your friends, family, coworkers or even your future spouse; you will deal with debt in your life. You must decide if you will let debt control your life. That decision starts now. According to Time.com, 73% of Americans will die with consumer debt. Reread that sentence and let it sink in. 73% of Americans let debt control their ENTIRE lives. You are going to be tempted, especially over the next 10 years, with flashy cars or new electronics. You need to decide if they are worth going into debt for.

Take Action

Take a minute to write down why you want to be smart about debt. You will learn more about debt in later chapters, but it is important to make the decision now. Do you want to give back? Avoid financial stress? Travel?

What Factors Should I Consider?

If you need to take out student loans, a mortgage or find yourself with medical debt, you will need to understand a few terms:

Interest Rate: The percentage of extra money paid to the borrower for the use of their money. For example, if you have a $100,000 loan with a 5% interest rate, if you paid nothing the first month you would owe $105,000. It is important that you pay attention to the interest rate of your loan because the higher the interest rate the longer it will take to pay off.

Principal Amount: The initial amount of the loan. It can also mean the amount remaining. For example, if you took out a $100,000 loan your principal amount is $100,000. If after 3 years the amount owed is $70,000 your new principal amount is $70,000.

Payment Terms: These terms specify how long you have to pay off the loan and any other specific requirements. For example, if you took out a $200,000 loan at 5% for a 30-year mortgage, your payment terms are 30 years. You must pay it back within 30 years.

For now, it is just important that you understand what debt is. I will explain in later chapters specific types of debt that might affect you in the near future. You might have to take out debt, student loans or a mortgage for a home, but you don't have to let it control your life.

PART TWO: TIME TO WORK

4. CREDIT CARDS

In 2017, 74.6% of Americans carried credit card debt.

Some people will tell you it's the devil in card form, others will tell you it's a useful tool. I am here to teach you what a credit card is and what it is not.

What It Is:
- It allows you to borrow money from a bank to make purchases
- It is a tool to get cash back or travel rewards
- It helps you build your credit score
- It is easier than carrying a stack of cash (in my opinion)

What It Is Not:
- You **do not** actually have the money
- You should never reach your credit limit if you do not have the money in your checking/savings account

- Missing payments or maxing out your credit card will lower your credit score
- Interest rates are normally extremely high (making a small debt a much larger debt)
- If you are not careful, you can overspend and end up in credit card debt

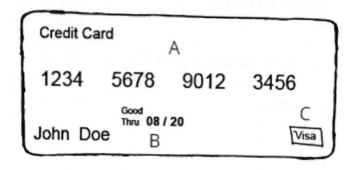

A: credit card number
B: expiration date
C: credit card company
D: security code

Wait, Interest Is Bad?

Well, depends on what you are referring to. In a previous chapter you learned how compound interest can work in your favor with savings accounts. That type of interest is good. Credit card interest, on the other hand, is the opposite. Instead of getting extra money, you are paying extra money. Credit card interest (also known as credit card APR) averages from 12% to 24%. That means you pay extra on your purchase. For example, you buy a $1,000 TV. If you do not pay it off within 25–30 days (depending on your credit card), your TV now costs $1,120-$1,240. If you continue not to pay, the amount goes up.

Your credit card company might say, "Oh, you just need to pay the minimum balance each month, no worries!" You say, "Wow, that is so amazing, I can pay $20 now and get a $1,000 TV! What a steal!"

If you have a $1,000 balance, your interest rate (APR) is 20%, and your minimum payment is $20. If you only pay your minimum payment, it will take you 194 months to pay off that TV and you will pay a total of $3,126! That is an extra $2,126 for that TV. If you paid off your credit card right away (or paid cash) you would be MUCH better off.

Another fun fact: your interest rate can INCREASE if you keep missing payments. Yes, that is correct.

There are many credit card balance calculators you can use, but I have a link to my favorite in the resources section of the book.

Take Action

Go to the resource section of the book and go to the BankRate minimum payment calculator. Try a few examples to see how much you'd pay if you only paid the minimum on your credit card.

For example: if you bought a $2,000 MacBook Pro on your credit card and paid the minimum of $30 a month with an interest rate of 22%, how long would it take you to pay it off and how much would it really cost?

So Why Should I Get a Credit Card?

Do you need a credit card? No. Is it a super useful tool when used correctly? 100% yes. I got a credit card at 18 years old (you need to be at least 18 years old to get a credit card by yourself). My dad told me to put small expenses on it each month. I started with gas or food and paid it off right away. I never had a balance, never paid interest, and never missed a payment. It is 100% possible to have a credit card and stay out of credit card debt if and only if you are determined and responsible.

You might be tempted with super cool sign-up bonuses or your favorite store might give you 20% off if you sign up for their card but **RESIST**. Resist the urge to sign up for every credit card offer you get. I promise they will ALL sound amazing and have some great discounts. You do not need 15 credit cards. That is an awful idea even if you do manage them responsibly.

I understand some people cannot be trusted with credit cards. Maybe that is you. If so that is totally fine, don't get one. If you can be trusted and you understand what they are, you can develop responsible credit card habits early and start building your credit score (which we will talk more about in the next chapter). I now use credit cards for pretty much everything. I rarely have cash (I know, gasp).

What Credit Card Should I Get?

For your first card, you want to make sure you choose one with no annual fee. There are some great options that have no annual fee, which means they do not cost you anything if you use them correctly. Remember, you need to be at least 18 years old to open a credit card so most of these are geared toward college students.

According to nerdwallet.com, the top credit cards for students in 2018 are:

Discover it for Students:
- Perfect for credit newbies

- No annual fee and no foreign transaction fee
- 1% cash back, 5% cash back at different places each quarter
- Good grades rewards ($20 cash back each school year your GPA is 3.0 or higher)
- Free FICO score
- Late payments do not increase your APR (but you still will pay interest)

Citi ThankYou Preferred Card for Students:

- 2,500 points are redeemable for $25 in gift cards, electronics, etc.
- 2x points on dining out and entertainment, 1 point/dollar for all other spending
- No annual fee but 3% foreign transaction fee (if you plan on studying abroad in college you might not want this one)

Journey Student Rewards from Capital One:

- Earn 1% cash back on all purchases
- Pay on time to boost your cash back to 1.25% for the month (always pay on time)
- No cash back limit & rewards do not expire
- No annual fee & no foreign transaction fees
- Don't have to be a student to apply (this is perfect if you are not a college student)

Take Action

Research the above cards as well as other cards with no annual fee and write down your top 2 cards. Write down the pros and cons of each.

Make Credit Cards Work for You Not Against You

If you decide you want to open a credit card, either now or in the future, here are some important things to remember:

1. ALWAYS pay on time and in full (if you ignore the rest of this chapter, please remember this).

2. Your credit card limit is not how much money you have. If your limit is $1,000, you do not have $1,000 to spend. The only money you have to spend is what is in your checking or savings account.

3. Do not be tempted by store offers or sign-up bonuses. Choose a credit card that works best for you and only open that ONE. The more cards you open the more you will be tempted to spend. Do not open a second card without a valid reason and until you have proven to yourself you can be trusted. Please make sure you understand this. You do not want to be someone with 15 credit

cards. That is NEVER a good idea.

4. Credit cards can be a useful tool if used responsibly. The key word is responsibly. Don't worry about what everyone else is doing. Statistics show they will end up in credit card debt at some point.

5. If you aren't sure if you will use it responsibly, don't open one.

6. Make sure to monitor your credit card online to see if the number was stolen. Hackers are crazy these days. They can get. your credit card or debit card number without getting your card. Make sure to keep track of your balance and account. If you find fraudulent charges, contact the bank immediately.

Only open a credit card if you have self-control and trust that you will use it correctly.

5. CREDIT SCORE

40 million Americans have a FICO credit score lower than 600.

Are you going to buy a house in the future? Rent an apartment? Pay your own utilities? If so, you need to care about your credit score. Credit scores are not only for buying a house anymore, rental companies and utilities companies are also checking credit scores.

A credit score is a three-digit number that estimates how likely you are to repay borrowed money. If you are making regular payments to a lender you probably have a credit score. A bad credit score is anything under 550. An excellent credit score is anything above 750. The bad part is if you ruin your credit score it does take some time to fix it. There is no instant fix. Side note: you don't need to pay someone to fix your credit score. This is why it is important to understand what it is, how it is determined, and how to increase it.

What Affects My Credit Score?

The top six factors that have an effect on your credit score are:

1. **Credit Card Utilization (high impact):**
   Amount of your total available credit you are currently using.
2. **Payment History (high impact):**
   The percentage of payments you've made on time.
3. **Derogatory Marks (high impact):**
   Collection accounts, bankruptcies, tax liens, etc.
4. **Age of Credit History (medium impact):**
   The average length of time your accounts have been open.
5. **Total Accounts (low impact):**
   Total number of open and closed accounts on your report.
6. **Credit Inquiries (low impact):**
   The number of hard inquiries on your credit report

Why Should I Really Care about My Credit Score?

Although you might be a few years away from

taking out any loans or opening credit cards, you need to understand why an excellent credit score is important.

Loan Interest Rates: An excellent credit score will help lower your interest rate on any type of loan. For example, if the interest percentage is 1–2% lower, the savings on interest payments over the life of a 15 or 30-year mortgage loan are substantial. You would save tens of thousands of dollars with a lower interest rate on a mortgage loan.

Ability to Negotiate: With an excellent credit score you can negotiate with lenders. You will be able to shop around for loans, credit cards, etc. instead of just taking anyone who will offer you a loan.

No Security Deposits: As I stated earlier, many utility companies require a security deposit for customers who have low credit scores. With an excellent credit score they will waive the deposit.

Credit Card Opportunities: Some of the cards with the best rewards require an excellent credit score. Of course, as I stated in the previous chapter, it is important to be responsible with your credit cards and pay the balance off each month.

Having a very low credit score or no credit score could be a major hassle when you are making big life decisions. Unless I win the lottery or somehow make millions super-fast I will not be able to pay for a house in cash. It is just not realistic for me. I will need a mortgage loan, which means they will evaluate my credit score to decide my interest rate. More than 43% of Americans don't know that having bad credit can negatively impact the price of car insurance. More than 52% of Americans don't know that it can negatively impact the cost of utility deposits (NerdWallet Study).

I Start Out with a Perfect Score, Right?

It is the opposite (I know it sucks). You start with no score at all and you have to build it. Unlike your math class there isn't any extra credit either. People think you start with a credit score of 0, but that isn't true. You just start with no score at all. If you haven't borrowed money you have no score. Don't worry though. This is not something you need to worry about at this moment, but it is something you should start thinking about.

Tips for Increasing Your Credit Score

If you find yourself with a low credit score because you missed some payments, you don't need to pay a credit repair company to help you increase your score. You can do it yourself. Follow these tips:

Open a Credit Card in College: The sooner you start building your credit score the easier it will be to buy a home or purchase in the future. It will also help you get better deals on apartments, utilities, car insurance, phone bills, etc. Review the credit card chapter for tips on how to use credit cards responsibly.

ALWAYS Pay on Time: This has one of the greatest effects on your score. You never want to miss a loan or credit card payment. As we discussed previously, you should always pay your entire credit card balance, but if you cannot you need to at least pay the minimum by the due date.

Check for Mistakes: Make sure to check your credit score once a month to make sure there are no mistakes. You can request your score for free once a year from each of the three credit bureaus. You can also use websites such as Credit Karma or Credit Sesame to check your credit score for free and they can send you alerts.

Keep Your Credit Utilization Under 30%: For example, if you have $3,000 of debt and $5,000 of available credit, your credit utilization is 60%. If you have $1000 of debt and $5,000 of available credit, your credit utilization is 20%. More than 41% of Americans think carrying a small balance on a credit card month to month can help improve a person's credit score (NerdWallet). This is NOT true. You do not need to carry debt to have a high credit score. I have an extremely high credit score and no debt.

You don't need to worry about your credit score right now because my guess is you have no score. This is perfectly normal for a high school student. I just want you to start thinking about what it is and how it is determined.

6. FINDING A JOB

In July 2017, there were 20.9 million employed 16- to 24-year-olds.

Now is the time to try different jobs and figure out what you like and what you don't. Maybe by babysitting you will learn you really do NOT want to be a teacher. Maybe by working in a restaurant you will learn you want to open your own one day because you see ways that things can get done more efficiently. High school is the perfect time to try out jobs in different sectors. I am not saying do it for a day and quit, please do NOT do that. Try it for a summer if it is seasonal or at least a few months if it is not. Forming good habits now will help you SO much in the long run, I promise.

Tips for Keeping Your Job:

1. **Be Respectful**: Respectful of your boss,

coworkers, customers. Just because you are in high school does not mean you should not take this job seriously.

2. **Be on Time:** This is a habit you need to get into ASAP. You should never be late for your job. You definitely will not want to be late when you have a full-time job. Set multiple alarms if you have to.

3. **Ask Questions:** If you are just starting out it is okay to ask questions and ask for help. It is better to ask in the beginning if you do not know than to wait 3–4 months and still have no idea what you are doing.

4. **Do More Than the Minimum:** Maybe you are just doing this for the paycheck. Trust me; I've been there. That doesn't mean you should just do the bare minimum. Take every opportunity as a learning lesson. You might not enjoy your job, but find one thing each day that you can learn from it. Try to help others, shadow your boss or see what else you can do.

5. **Network:** You might be thinking, *Umm, I am 16 and I work in a restaurant, who am I networking with?* Network with your customers, with your boss, and with your coworkers. You never know when you

might need their help. For real, networking is KEY.

Take Action

Write down 1–2 things you can do at your job each day to help you grow. It could be helping in another area, shadowing your boss, asking for customer feedback, asking your coworkers what you could do to help them, etc.

Seasonal Job Options:

Seasonal jobs are great, especially during the holidays and summer. Maybe you don't have time for a part-time job all year long because of school obligations or after school activities. You have to keep your grades up! Seasonal jobs are a great way to get work experience and some extra money without the yearlong commitment. Some seasonal job options are:

- Camp Counselor
- Retail Store (they always need extra help around the holidays)
- Summer Tutor
- Lifeguard
- Golf Course Caddy
- Babysitter
- Dogwalker/Pet-sitter
- Job Shadow

Year-Round Job Options:

If you can manage your school work and after school activities, try to find a year-round job. These are a GREAT way to get experience for college applications, future jobs, and building references. Some year-round job options are:

- Retail Store
- Restaurant
- Babysitter
- Tutoring
- Dogwalker/Pet-sitter
- Front Desk Receptionist
- Grocery Store
- Movie Theater Cashier/Usher

Where Can I Find Jobs?

I am so glad you asked! There are many different places to find jobs so make sure to try a few. Apply to multiple jobs and if you hear back from a few that is great, now you have options! Don't know where to apply? Below are some ideas to get you started.

- Online Job Websites
- Indeed.com
- Snagajob.com
- Monster.com
- Company Website

- Ask Family or Friends
- Ask Your School Counselor
- Put Flyers in Mailboxes
- In Person

I actually made flyers in high school and put them in my neighbors' mailboxes for a babysitting job. I wrote my age, why I am qualified, how they could reach me (my house phone number—yes, I am OLD), and what job I was looking for. I got 2 different babysitting jobs from those flyers. If you need help finding a job, ask your parents. They might know someone who is looking for help or other places to apply. Don't give up!

Take Action
Write down 1–2 possible jobs, where you will apply (company website, job website, in person, etc.), and the date you will apply by.

7. GETTING YOUR FIRST PAYCHECK

78% of U.S. workers live paycheck to paycheck to make ends meet.

Congrats on your first job! I bet you are super excited to get your first real paycheck. There are few things you need to understand first.

How Often Are You Getting Paid?

Unless you are babysitting or tutoring you most likely will not get paid every day you work. If you are working at a restaurant or a retail store, you might get paid weekly, biweekly or once a month (depending on the establishment). Make sure you know before you start how often you are getting paid so you can make a plan and a budget.

How Are You Getting Paid?

Depending on your job you might get paid in cash, by check or by direct deposit.

Cash: Usually babysitting, tutoring or tips. Make sure you put this cash in a bank account so you can keep track and also effectively manage your money.

Check: You might receive a check each week, biweekly or monthly from your employer. You can deposit this check into your checking or savings account by going to the bank, using an ATM or using your bank's phone app.

Direct Deposit: Your employer might deposit your paycheck directly into your bank account. This would be set up before you start working there and you would have to provide your employer with the routing and account number for your checking account. Your paycheck would automatically be deposited into your account weekly, biweekly or monthly. This is how my paycheck is set up for work.

Take Action
Open the calendar app on your phone or get a planner and write down when you will be getting paid so you can keep track.

Things to Remember:

1. Start brainstorming events or things you might need to save for
2. Talk to your parents about where you should put your money: what bank, checking vs. savings
3. Make sure you talk to your employer about how often you are getting paid and what the form of payment is
4. If you are an hourly employee and you do not work the same number of hours each week, your paycheck might not always be the same. This is important to remember when budgeting

Getting your first "real" job and first paycheck is super exciting, but remember you didn't work this hard to spend your entire paycheck. Before you buy something, think of how many hours you had to work to buy it. That has helped me a TON. If you make $15/hour and you want to buy a $300 item that means you had to work 20 hours just to afford that one item. This might stop you from buying it or at least will make you think.

Take Action

Write down 3 things you want to buy and calculate how many hours you have to work to buy them. Keep this in your planner or on your phone to remind you how many hours they really cost.

In the next chapter we will go over setting up your first budget and what you should include. Even though you might not have a ton of expenses right now, it is important to understand what you should include in a budget and get in the habit of budgeting.

8. BUDGET

According to the 2016 US Bank Possibility Index, 59% of Americans did not have a budget.

You might not want to set up a budget. You might think it takes too much time or that it's too "adult" for you and you don't want to worry about that right now. The truth is a budget is just telling your money where to go instead of wondering where it went. It shouldn't take you too long to set up and getting in the habit young will help you in the future.

What Is a Budget?

A budget is an estimate of your income and expenses for that month. You break up your expenses into different categories: rent, utilities, Netflix, loans, etc. There are different types of budgets, but I recommend a zero-based budget.

This just means income-outgoing = zero. You should allocate every dollar you spend. This does not mean all of it goes to expenses but it can also include giving/tithing and saving.

Zero-Based Budget Example:

Below is an example of a zero-based budget. This is a monthly budget, but if you get paid weekly or biweekly you can also do a weekly or biweekly budget as well as a monthly overview budget.

Income after Taxes	$500
Gas	$80
Going Out	$100
Netflix	$10
Clothes	$40
Expenses Total	$230
Christmas Gifts	$90
General Savings	$100
Prom	$30
Birthday Gifts	$50
Savings Total	$270
What's Left	$0

You can see at the end of the month you have $0 left. This is good. This means you allocated every dollar you have to an expense or a savings goal.

Other Expenses:

You might have to pay for other expenses besides going out with friends, gas, and clothes. Some other expenses you might have are:

- Cell Phone Bill
- Weekend Plans/Trips
- Beauty Products
- Video Games
- Date Nights
- In Case of Emergency

What Should I Save For?

Getting in the habit of saving money is so important. You might think you don't need to save right now, but I promise you do. The more you save in high school the better off you will be. Some things you should be saving for are:

- Gifts
- Prom
- Buying a Car
- College expenses
- After-graduation trip
- Spring Break
- Cell phone
- New clothes
- Electronics or video games

Take Action
Write down 5 things you want to save for and talk to your parents to see if you are forgetting anything.

Creating Your Budget

There are many different ways to create a budget depending on your organizational style and what works for you.

Excel: You can create an excel file for your budget with your income minus expenses and savings. If you are tech-savvy this might be more appealing to you. You can even do this on Google docs so you can view/edit your budget on your phone. You can create a very simple excel budget or there are some great excel templates online.

Pen/Paper: You might be old school and prefer writing your budget. You can keep it in a notebook or on a piece of paper in a folder.

Phone App/Website: There are some great phone apps and websites to help you budget. Some are free and some have a monthly fee. I recommend using a free app/website for now since your budget will be pretty simple and you don't have too many expenses. Some free apps/websites are EveryDollar and Mint. Another good budgeting app is You Need a Budget, but it is only free for one month and then you have to pay.

Take Action

Fill in the budget template below to get started creating your budget. Transfer this budget to excel, paper or a phone app.

Income (weekly, biweekly, or monthly)	
Expense 1:	
Expense 2:	
Expense 3:	
Savings Goal 1:	
Savings Goal 2:	
Savings Goal 3:	

Budgeting Tips

1. Review your budget at least once a month to make sure you don't need to change anything.
2. If your income changes, adjust your budget.
3. Ask for help if you need it: email us at admin@financiallifocused.com if you need help with your budget.
4. Be honest or your budget will not work: if you normally spend $100/mo on going out with friends do not write in your budget that you will spend $50/mo. This is not helpful and the only person you are hurting is yourself.
5. Keep your budget in a place where you will actually see it: if you are always on your

phone maybe you want your budget on your phone. Don't write it on a piece of paper, stick it in a drawer, and forget where it is.

If you don't have many monthly expenses that is great. That means you can allocate your paycheck to saving and giving. Make sure you set savings goals to keep you motivated. If you need $600 for prom in June and you are starting to save in January, try to save $100 a month for prom. Make sure it is in a prom category so you don't use that money for something else. You can open multiple savings accounts for different categories or keep the cash in envelopes labeled prom, car, etc.

Your budget is a tool that will help you effectively manage your money. The sooner you get in the habit of budgeting the easier it will be when you have more expenses and savings goals.

9. TAXES

57% of Americans do not understand the current tax code.

Taxes. This is not a topic your parents, coworkers or friends will be thrilled to talk about. Who wants to lose money from their paycheck each month? No one I know. Since you will be losing money from your paycheck for taxes it is important that you understand what they are and where they go (the basics since we really don't know exactly).

What Are Taxes?

On each paycheck you will notice that your employer has withheld (taken out) the taxes you owe. Taxes are payments of money to the government. Taxes are used for national defense, roads, street lights, highways, social security, Medicare/Medicaid, etc.

There are federal income taxes and possibly state and local income taxes depending on where you live. Your taxes go to a variety of different departments within the government.

Federal Income Taxes: Social Security, Medicaid, Medicare, defense, education, social services, national parks, and unemployment.

State and Local Taxes: Education, health insurance, corrections, higher education, roads, highways, and public assistance.

As of 2018, there are nine states in the US that have no income tax. Alaska, Florida, Nevada, New Hampshire, South Dakota, Tennessee, Texas, Washington, and Wyoming have no income tax for residents. If you live in one of these states you still will pay federal income tax.

How Does This Affect My Job?

When you start a new job, your employer will have you complete a document called a W-4. This is the Employee's Withholding Allowance Certificate. This helps your employer determine how much money to withhold from your wages for taxes. Your parents can help you fill out this form if you have questions.

Each year your employer will send you a document called a W-2. This is a Wage and Tax Statement that shows how much you earned in wages and how much you paid in state and federal taxes. You need this form when you file your tax return. You will insert the information into the tax software you use to determine what you owe in taxes or what you get back from the government. Your parents or a tax professional can help you complete your tax return. TurboTax and H&R Block have online software you can use for free or relatively cheaply.

Take Action

Research your own state and see where state taxes went last year. Look at the percentages to see where the largest amount went.

Tax Tips

1. Make sure to complete your budget using your after-tax income.
2. If you have any specific questions about tax withholdings make sure to talk to your employer or parents.
3. Don't forget to file your taxes each year.

PART THREE:
LIFE AFTER
HIGH SCHOOL

10. CHOOSING YOUR PATH

As of 2016, 41% of students seeking a bachelor's degree at a four year institution did not graduate within 6 years.

It's time to decide what you will do after you graduate high school. You are probably used to adults telling you what to do your entire life and making all the important decisions for you. That time is up. It is time for you to step up and take responsibility for yourself. You might be thinking, *I've made important decisions before.* Not like this. This decision is more important than the party you attend on Friday night or the date that you take to prom. So give this decision some respect. Do your research, sit down and talk about it with a trusted adult, and take some time to think about your options. Don't feel like you have to do what everyone else at your high school is doing. So they are going to a four-year school? Cool. That might not be the right choice for you. There are so many options out there. The first step to making any responsible decision is to get educated.

Take Action
Make a list of your strengths and weaknesses. Use this list to help you decide on possible career paths.

In-State vs. Out of State

In-State:

Pros	Cons
In-state tuition is less expensive	Fewer schools/ programs to choose
Lower travel costs to get home	Being around the same people from your high school

Out of State:

Pros	Cons
More options for schools/majors	Out-of-state tuition is more expensive
Experience new place and culture	Higher cost to travel home

Private vs. Public University

When deciding whether you want to attend a public or private university, think about what you value. Do you value having strong relationships with professors and classmates or are you more interested in sports, extracurriculars and the college lifestyle? Ask yourself what is more important prestige or low cost? Smaller classes or a wider variety of courses?

Private:

Pros	Cons
Smaller classes	More expensive
Tight Knit Community	Low acceptance rates
Prestigious	Fewer majors and classes

Public:

Pros	Cons
Less expensive	Larger classes
More activities, clubs, sports	Less face time with professors
Many majors and classes	Prioritize in-state students

When deciding whether you want to attend a public or private university, think about what you value. Do you value having strong relationships with professors and classmates or are you more interested in sports, extracurriculars and the college lifestyle? Ask yourself what is more important prestige or low cost? Smaller classes or a wider variety of courses?

Most of the time the decision comes down to cost. Although private universities are generally much more expensive than public universities, they do offer prospective students substantial merit-based scholarships. So if your heart is set on a private school, then you should apply and see if you qualify for a scholarship based on your grades, GPA, and test scores.

Community College

If you are on a really tight budget consider going to community college for two years then transferring to a four-year university. Community colleges tend to be much less expensive compared to other schools and they offer you the opportunity to take the core classes needed for most majors. Just be sure to do your research if you plan to transfer after two years. You will need to double-check that the university you want to transfer to will accept credits from your local community college. Nobody has time to do all that work for nothing.

You can also attend a community college to get your associate's degree. Most people think that you can't make a good living with a two-year degree; this is totally false! You can get a well-respected and decent paying job after just two years of college. Here are some examples:

- Pharmacy Tech
- Dental Hygienist
- Radiology Technician
- Paralegal
- Physical Therapy Assistant
- Computer Science

Trade School

You might be thinking that college is not right for you. That is totally fine, but furthering your education doesn't have to be all about reading textbooks and taking exams.

If school isn't your thing but you want to get a good job, consider going to a trade school. Trade schools provide you with the skills and training that you need to get a specific job. You could study to become a cosmetologist, electrician, plumber, mechanic or welder.

11. FINANCIAL AID

In 2017, the total student loan debt in the United States was more than 1.3 trillion.

Let's be honest, student loans suck. But sometimes they are necessary. If you are planning to go to college, and like many of us you don't have a college fund or full ride, then chances are you will need to accept some student loans. The most important thing to remember about student loans is that they are not free money. You have to pay them back with interest!

Getting Financial Aid

In order to be eligible for loans or grants for college you must complete the FAFSA (Free Application for Federal Student Aid). You can complete the FAFSA online at FAFSA.gov. The FAFSA opens each year on October 1st. When completing your

FAFSA be sure to enter each of the schools that you have applied to or will be applying to so that their financial aid offices will be sent your information.

You will need a few things to be able to complete the FAFSA:

- Social Security Number
- Your federal income tax returns, W-2s or other records of money earned (if you have worked)
- Bank statements and records of investments (if applicable)
- Records of untaxed income (if applicable)
- If you live with your parents and are considered a dependent student then you will need most of the information above for them as well

You will need to create a Federal Student Aid ID (FSA ID) to sign your FAFSA. You can create the FSA ID at the end of your FAFSA application on the signing page by clicking "Create FSA ID". You will then be taken to a separate window to enter your information and create your ID and password. Be sure to keep your ID and password somewhere safe because you will need them in the future.

Immediately after submitting your FAFSA you will be given an estimate on the amount of loans and grants you are eligible for; however, you will have to wait for each college's financial aid office to contact you for the actual amount. After getting accepted into college, your college's financial aid office will notify you of the amount of school-based scholarships and federal grants/loans you have been awarded. Scholarships and grants are great because you are not required to pay them back (unless you fail/drop out, then you will most likely have to pay a portion back). You will have to pay all of your student loans back. Every single penny. No matter what.

Grant
- Do not pay back
- No interest
- Based on your family's income
- Apply on FAFSA

Loan
- Must pay back
- Will pay interest
- Based on family's income
- Apply on FAFSA

School-Based Scholarship
- Do not pay back
- No interest
- Based on grades/GPA
- College will automatically award

Outside Scholarship
- Do not pay back
- No interest
- Based on many categories
- You must find and apply on your own

Accepting Your Loans

Once you have decided which college you will attend and signed up for classes, you will be able to log into your student account and see how much money you owe for tuition, housing, meal plan, etc. You will also see your scholarships/grants and have the option to accept or decline your student loans. It is very important for you to calculate how much money you will need each semester to pay for all of your expenses related to school.

Expenses you should calculate:
- Tuition
- Housing
- School Fees
- Meal Plan
- Gas
- Textbooks
- Any other bills you are responsible for

If you have been offered more financial aid than you need, you should decline some of your loans so that you do not spend them only to have to pay them back later with interest. Student loans should only be used for school related costs or living costs that are 100 percent necessary. You should not be spending your loans on spring break trips, electronics or nights out with friends. Believe me; you will regret it later if you spend your loans on senseless wants.

Take Action

Calculate the total cost for each semester. Next, calculate all of the scholarships, student loans and grants you have been awarded, plus any savings you will be using. Finally, subtract the costs from the funds to find out the amount of loans you can decline.

Costs	Funds
Tuition, Fees, Books	Scholarships
Housing	Grants
Meal Plan	Loans
Bills, Gas, Etc.	Savings
Total:	Total:

So which loans should you decline? You will most likely be offered several different kinds of student loans. They are not all the same. Some loans are better than others. There are three types of loans that may be awarded to you by the federal government.

Subsidized Stafford Loan: Is awarded based on financial need. Interest does not accrue while you are in school. Interest rates vary.

Federal Perkins Loan: Awarded based on financial need. Interest does not accrue while you are in school. The interest rate for all Perkins Loans is 5%.

Unsubsidized Stafford Loan: Available to any student. Interest accrues while you are in school. Interest rates vary.

If you have been offered an Unsubsidized Stafford Loan, you should decline this loan (or a portion of this loan) first if you do not need it. This is because interest will be accumulating while you are in school (bad interest!). You do not want to pay extra interest if you do not have to. If you have been offered more than one Unsubsidized Stafford Loan then you should compare the interest rates. You should always decline the Unsubsidized Loan with the highest interest rate first.

If you do not have any Unsubsidized Loans or if you need to decline even more loans, then you should compare the interest rates on your Subsidized Stafford Loans and Perkins Loans (if you have one). Decline the loans with the highest interest rate.

Remember to accept the loans that you do need! This chapter is not designed to discourage you from taking out loans to further your education. The purpose of this chapter is to give you knowledge of the student loan process and to keep you from spending your loans on unnecessary expenses. Your objective should be to take out the least amount of loans possible while still being able to graduate with your desired degree/certification.

12. SCHOLARSHIPS

For the 2014–15 school year, college students were awarded a total of $123.8 billion in scholarships and grants.

Scholarships don't just magically drop into your lap. You have to work for them. Some scholarships require you to write essays while others will review your past grades, volunteer hours or leadership skills. If you are hoping to pay for some of your education with scholarships then you need to get to work.

Build Your Scholarship Resume

You want a scholarship? Cool. So does everyone else. If you have good grades, that's awesome! But a lot of scholarships take more into account than your grades or test scores. You need to be able to answer this question: Why do I deserve to have someone else pay for my education? There are so many things that you can do to build you scholarship resume:

- Volunteer
- Join a club or sports team
- Get a job
- Run for student government
- Help others
- Ask your teachers for references
- Attend a writing workshop to improve your essay writing

Types of Scholarships

Many states offer scholarships to students who attend a school within their home state. These scholarships are based on grades, test scores and GPA. For example, as of 2017, the following states have Education Lottery scholarships: Arkansas, Florida, Georgia, Kentucky, New Mexico, South Carolina, West Virginia, and Tennessee. Do some research to see if your state offers any scholarships.

The college or university you attend may also offer you a merit based scholarship. Some of these are awarded automatically and some you will need to apply for. If your heart is set on moving as far away from your parents as possible (I don't blame you ... just kidding, Mom!) then you will be happy to know that many colleges offer in-state tuition to students from out of state. So go ahead and apply to your dream school that is across the country because you may get offered in-state tuition!

Outside organizations also offer scholarships for students. You will need to find these scholarships on your own. Yes, you will be required to do some research. And yes, you will probably have to write an essay, but it will be worth it in the long run.

Where to Find Scholarships

There are hundreds of thousands of scholarships out there so you would think that it would be easy to find scholarships to apply for, right? Wrong. Many of these scholarships are very specific to certain majors, groups or states. Because there are so many super specific scholarships it takes a long time to find just one scholarship that is applicable to you. It can be hard to know where to start when looking for scholarships so here is a list of the best places to start your scholarship search:

The College Board Scholarship Search:
A database that allows you to enter your information and then matches you with relevant scholarships. The link can be found in the resource section in the back of the book.

Your High School Counselor:
Your high school counselor is a scholarship expert! Ask your counselor if you can sit down and discuss

possible scholarships to apply for.

Your College's Financial Aid Website:
Be sure to check out your college's financial aid website to see what scholarships are offered by the school and which outside scholarships they recommend. Some colleges will give you the opportunity to apply for scholarships during the application process, others allow you to apply for scholarships based on your major after your freshman or sophomore year. If your school counselor is a scholarship expert then your college financial aid workers are the scholarship gurus, so be sure to contact them if you need more information.

Organization or Club:
If you are a member of an organization or club find out if they offer a scholarship. For example, JROTC and The National Honor Society both offer scholarships to some of their members.

Take Action
Set aside an hour and visit some of the scholarship resources listed above. Write down 3–4 scholarships you might want to apply for and what they are looking for (grades, volunteering, organizations, etc.) Discuss this list with your parents/school counselor to make sure you are on track to meet the requirements and deadlines.

Be proactive! Do not wait until the last minute of your senior year to apply for scholarships! And remember, you can lose your scholarship if you do not maintain your GPA or fulfill any other requirements.

CONCLUSION

You finished the book! It is okay if you are a little overwhelmed. We threw A LOT of information at you. Keep this book as a resource and PLEASE refer back to it as needed. If you have specific questions, please email us. We would love to help you.

We included "Take Action" prompts throughout the book so we hope you took some time to complete them. This book isn't like the required book in your English class. Do not speed through it just to get to the end to tell your parents/teacher you read it. Take time to reread chapters, do the "Take Action" prompts, and discuss it with your parents, friends, or legal guardian.

Our goal for Not Another Money Statistic is to empower others to take control of their finances early and not become another statistic. In the back of the book are checklists that highlight the important steps you need to take.

You now have the tools you need to successfully manage your finances. We hope you remember us when you save your first million.

NOTES

2015 FDIC National Survey of Unbanked and Underbanked Households." *EconomicInclusion.gov,* 20 Oct. 2016, www.economicinclusion.gov/.

"2016 U.S. Bank Possibility Index." *2016 U.S. Bank Possibility Index,* U.S. Bank, stories.usbank.com/dam/possibilityindex/USBankPossibilityIndex.pdf.

"As IRS Opens, Taxpayers Stressed Over Filing but Thinking About Refunds." *PR Newswire: News Distribution, Targeting and Monitoring,* 29 Jan. 2018, www.prnewswire.com/news-releases/as-irs-opens-taxpayers-stressed-over-filing-but-thinking-about-refunds-300589272.html.

"Board of Governors of the Federal Reserve System." *The Fed - Consumer Credit - G.19,* 7 Mar. 2018, www.federalreserve.gov/releases/g19/current/.

Calfas, Jennifer. "Majority of Americans Die in Debt | Money." *Time,* Time, 22 Mar. 2017, time.com/money/4709270/americans-die-in-debt/.

"Employment and Unemployment Among Youth Summary." *U.S. Bureau of Labor Statistics,* U.S. Bureau of Labor Statistics, 16 Aug. 2017, www.bls.gov/news.release/youth.nr0.htm.

"Federal Student Loan Portfolio." *Federal Student Aid,* 8 Mar. 2018, studentaid.ed.gov/sa/about/data-center/student/portfolio.

"Grants & Scholarships." *An Overview of College Grants and Scholarships*, bigfuture.collegeboard.org/pay-for-college/grants-scholarships.

Issa, Erin El. "How Costly Is Bad Credit? Many Don't Know, Survey Shows." *NerdWallet*, 24 May 2017, www.nerdwallet.com/blog/finance/bad-credit-score-survey/.

"Living Paycheck to Paycheck Is a Way of Life for Majority of U.S. Workers, According to New CareerBuilder Survey." *Press Room | Career Builder*, press.careerbuilder.com/2017-08-24-Living-Paycheck-to-Paycheck-is-a-Way-of-Life-for-Majority-of-U-S-Workers-According-to-New-CareerBuilder-Survey.

"Percent with Debt." *Consumer Credit Explorer*, Philadelphia Federal Reserve, www.philadelphiafed.org/eqfx/webstat/index.

The Condition of Education - Postsecondary Education - Programs, Courses, and Completions - Undergraduate Retention and Graduation Rates - Indicator April (2017), nces.ed.gov/programs/coe/indicator_ctr.asp.

United States, Congress, "Report on the Economic Well-Being of U.S Households in 2016." *Report on the Economic Well-Being of U.S Households in 2016*, May 2017. www.federalreserve.gov/publications/files/2016-report-economic-well-being-us-households-201705.pdf.

CHECKLISTS

Maybe you don't have time to go through an entire chapter but you want to go back and see exactly what you need to do. That is what the checklists are for. The next few pages contain the most important to-dos from each chapter of the book. The checklist is just a cheat-sheet but does not contain everything you need to know. That is why we placed it at the end of the book. We know you might like to take the shortcut and jump to the end and see what you have to do but sadly there are no shortcuts for effectively managing your finances. It takes time, motivation, and education.

Okay we are done ranting about the importance of personal finance. Get started on the checklists!

Chapter 1: Checking Account

- ☐ Compare different checking accounts (make pros and cons list)
- ☐ Talk to your parents or guardian about the different options
- ☐ Open a checking account and make an initial deposit

Chapter 2: Savings Account

- ☐ Compare different savings accounts
- ☐ Talk to your parents or guardian about the different options
- ☐ Open a savings account and make an initial deposit
- ☐ Make a list of things you want to save for (include the amount and date)

Chapter 4: Credit Cards

- ☐ Use the BankRate minimum payment calculator to see how much an item would cost if you only paid the minimum on your credit card
- ☐ Talk to your parents or guardian about their thoughts on credit cards
- ☐ Compare different credit cards to decide which is best for you (if you decide to open one)

Chapter 6: Finding a Job

- ☐ Create a list of possible job options and where you will apply

- ☐ Write down the date you will apply by
- ☐ Write down 1–2 things you can do at your job each day to help you grow

Chapter 7: First Paycheck
- ☐ Open the calendar app on your phone or get a planner and write down when you will be getting paid so you can keep track.
- ☐ Write down 3 things you want to buy and calculate how many hours you have to work to buy them.

Chapter 8: Budget
- ☐ Fill in the table below (income = expenses + savings goals):

Income (weekly, biweekly, or monthly)	
Expense 1:	
Expense 2:	
Expense 3:	
Savings Goal 1:	
Savings Goal 2:	
Savings Goal 3:	

- ☐ Transfer your budget to an excel file, a notebook, or a phone app

Chapter 10: Choosing Your Path
- ☐ Research different career paths and write down ones that interest you
- ☐ Based on your career interests, make a list

of possible majors or certificate programs
- ☐ Make a list of schools that offer those majors or certificate programs
- ☐ Compare and contrast the schools to find one that is right for you (location, price, size)

Chapter 11/12: Financial Aid/Scholarships

- ☐ Talk to your parents or guardian about paying for college
- ☐ If you need financial aid, fill out the FAFSA application your senior year of high school
- ☐ Apply for applicable scholarships
- ☐ Calculate the estimated total cost of your first year of college
- ☐ Accept necessary financial aid

HELPFUL RESOURCES

Below are some resources we mentioned in the book and a few others to help you make money moves and not become another money statistic.

Credit Cards & Credit Scores

Credit Card Minimum Payment Calculator:
https://www.bankrate.com/calculators/credit-cards/credit-card-minimum-payment.aspx

Top Credit Cards for Students:
https://www.nerdwallet.com/blog/top-credit-cards/nerdwallets-best-college-student-credit-cards/

Credit Karma: https://www.creditkarma.com/

Budgeting

Mint: https://www.mint.com/

Zero-Based Budgeting:
https://www.daveramsey.com/blog/how-to-make-a-zero-based-budget

Clarity Money: https://claritymoney.com/

Paying for College

FAFSA: https://fafsa.gov/

Big Future Scholarship Search:
https://bigfuture.collegeboard.org/scholarship-search

Financial Aid Tools and Calculators:
https://bigfuture.collegeboard.org/pay-for-college/tools-calculators

WHAT'S NEXT

Not Another Money Statistic: Lessons We Wish We Learned in College

Overwhelmed by the cost of textbooks, going out with friends, and finding a full-time job? You'll learn how to live frugally, find an internship, and prepare for life after college.

Not Another Money Statistic: Lessons You Need to Know in Your Twenties

401k. Roth IRA. Health Savings Account. W2. If these terms aren't familiar to you, don't worry. You'll learn how to file taxes, save for retirement, pay off student loans, and more.

Visit **www.financiallifocused.com/nams** to be notified of future book releases.

ABOUT THE AUTHORS

We met at the University of South Carolina in 2009 and instantly became BFF. Shelly is the adventurous one and Alli is more Type A, but we complement each other pretty well. We have traveled the world together, started blogs together, and wrote our first book together.

Alli works for a Fortune 500 company and is pursuing her MBA in Finance. She runs the blog financiALLI focused and loves everything personal finance related. She is obsessed with the University of South Carolina (Go Gamecocks!) and studied abroad in China and Europe.

Shelly is a school social worker and has her Masters in Social Work from Washington University in St. Louis. She runs the blog The Eclectic Voyager and has been to 5 continents and over 15 countries. She is a certified scuba diver and has swam with 5 types of sharks.

We wrote this book together because we have different stories and opinions but the one thing we have in common is we want YOU to stay out of debt and understand your finance.

Made in the USA
San Bernardino, CA
06 July 2018